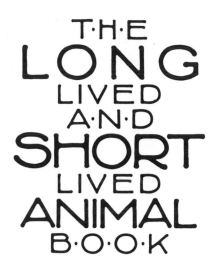

THE LONG LIVED AND SHORT LIVED ANIMAL BOOK

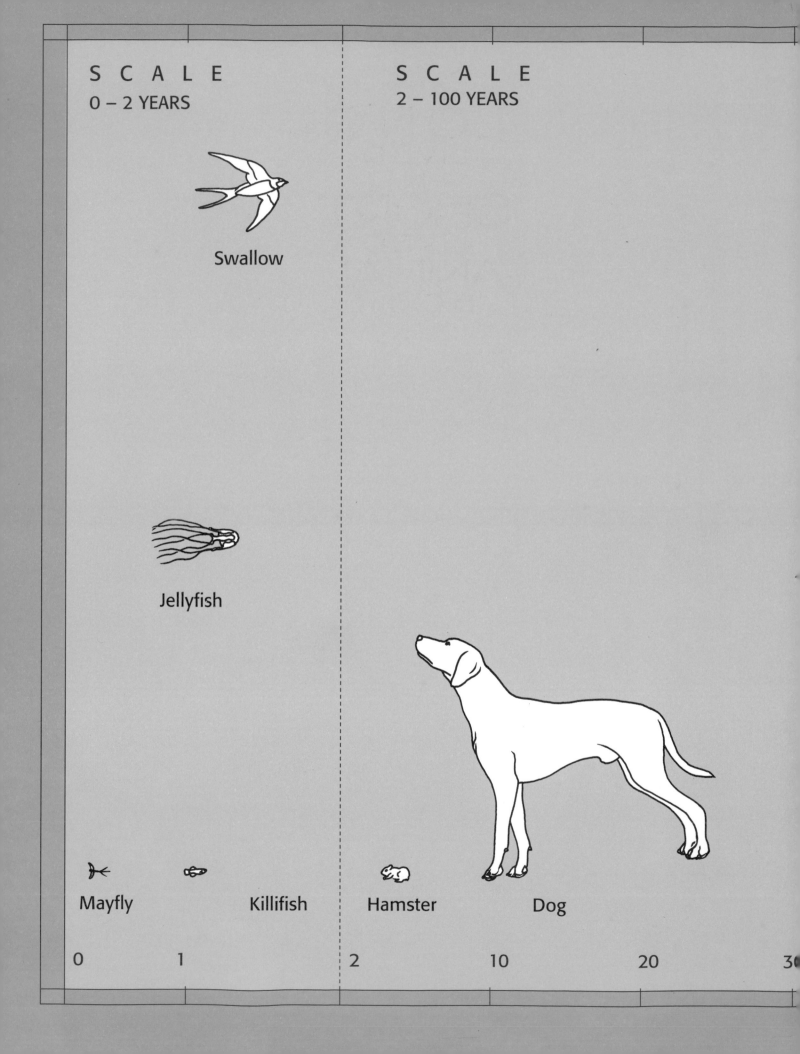

SCALE
0 – 2 YEARS

SCALE
2 – 100 YEARS

Swallow

Jellyfish

Mayfly

Killifish

Hamster

Dog

0   1   2   10   20   3[0]

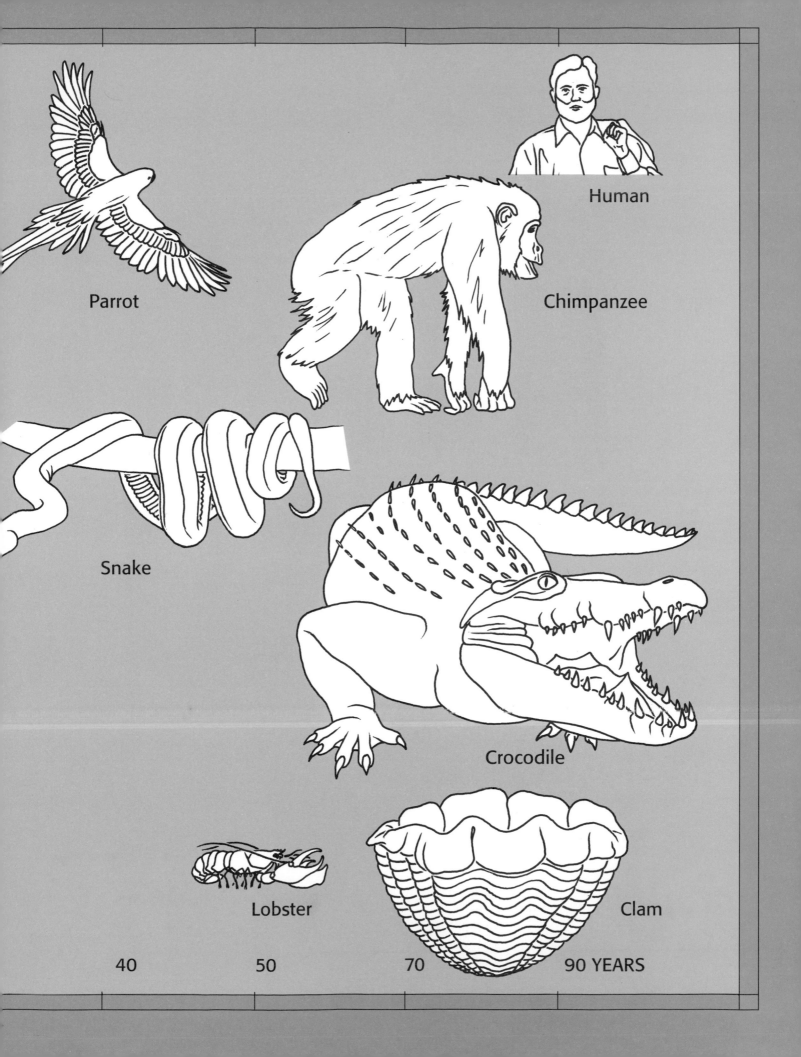

Parrot

Chimpanzee

Human

Snake

Crocodile

Lobster

Clam

40   50   70   90 YEARS

T·H·E
LONG
LIVED
A·N·D
SHORT
LIVED
ANIMAL
B·O·O·K

DAVID TAYLOR
ILLUSTRATED BY
PETER MASSEY

RSVP

RAINTREE
STECK-VAUGHN
P·U·B·L·I·S·H·E·R·S
The Steck-Vaughn Company

Austin, Texas

Contents

Words found in **bold** are explained in the glossary on page 31.

© Copyright 1996, this edition, Steck-Vaughn Company

All rights reserved. No part of this book may be reproduced or utilized in any form or by any means, electronic or mechanical, including photocopying, recording, or by any information storage and retrieval system, without permission in writing from the Publisher. Inquiries should be addressed to:

Copyright Permissions, Steck-Vaughn Company, P.O. Box 26015, Austin, TX 78755.

Published by Raintree Steck-Vaughn Publishers, an imprint of Steck-Vaughn Company

Illustration copyright © Peter Massey 1995
Text copyright © David Taylor 1995

Editor: Claire Edwards
Science Editor: Tracey Cohen
Electronic Production: Scott Melcer
Designer: Hayley Cove and Julie Klaus
Consultant: Fiona Collins

Library of Congress
Cataloging in Publication Data

Taylor, David, 1934–
    The long lived and short lived animal book / David Taylor; illustrated by Peter Massey.
        p.   cm. — (Animal opposites)
    Includes index.
    ISBN 0-8172-3952-9
    1. Animals—Juvenile literature. 2. Animal life spans—Juvenile literature. 3. Animal life cycles—Juvenile literarture. [1. Animals. 2. Animal life spans. 3. Animal life cycles.] I. Massey, Peter, ill. II. Title. III. Series: Taylor, David, 1934– Animal opposites.
QL49.T222   1996
591—dc20   95-6729
                                                  CIP   AC

Printed in Hong Kong.
Bound in the United States.
1 2 3 4 5 6 7 8 9 0 LB 99 98 97 96 95

Long-Lived and Short-Lived Animals

We all hope for a long and happy life. But what is a long life? Life is the period of time between birth and death. We measure it in units of time—years, months, days, hours, and minutes. The **life span** of animals varies greatly depending upon the **species**. Some big animals live a very long time. Elephants live for 60 years in the wild and more than 80 years in zoos. Giant tortoises live for 100, perhaps even 200 years. The shortest-living mammal is the forest shrew, which lives for less than a year. But tiny creatures can also live a long time. Queen termites have been known to lay eggs for up to 50 years.

Animals that have large numbers of young over a short period of time usually don't live long. If they did, the Earth might be overrun by mice or houseflies!

Scientists believe that the longest a human being can possibly live is around 113 years. Claims are sometimes made about a person living an amazing length of time. For instance, the Chinese person named, Li Chung-Yun, who died in 1933, was said to have lived for an astounding 253 years. Such claims have never been proved. The human life span varies, depending on where you live in the world. Life span also varies with sex. Women usually live longer than men do. On average, the life span for humans is about 75 years.

Life Span and Heartbeats

Every animal's heart beats about 800 million times during its lifetime. The total number of heartbeats during the life of both short-lived and long-lived species is roughly the same. This means that animals with short lives, such as mice and small birds, have hearts that beat very fast. The hearts of longer-lived animals, such as elephants and tortoises, beat much slower. Human beings are an exception. Our hearts beat almost 3 billion times in an average lifetime.

How Do We Grow?

All animals and plants are made of **microscopic** building blocks called **cells**. These multiply by dividing into two daughter cells. The two daughter cells divide when they are old enough. The continual production of cells is how the body renews itself and how we grow when we are young. Cells do not live as long as the body as a whole. They live, die, and are replaced by new cells. If this went on forever, the body would never die. But after a time, cells weaken, slow down, and often begin to behave in unusual ways.

As animals grow old, their cells age in a way that you can sometimes see. Human skin becomes more wrinkled, and hair changes color as it loses **pigment** and grows white or gray. Old chimpanzees and dogs often have white hairs around their faces, too.

Some forms of life, such as **bacteria**, are made of only one cell. These multiply by splitting into two, the two into four, and so on. Some can go on splitting like this every 20 minutes, and a single **bacterium** can multiply to become a million bacteria in less than eight hours! So you could say that the life of a bacterium is 20 minutes. Or, that because it goes on dividing, the cell lives forever. Both statements are correct.

A Look at Ages

Now let's return to animals we can see without a microscope. This book takes examples from across the animal kingdom and looks at how long they live in comparison with each other and with human beings. The animals in this book appear in order of how long they live. It starts with the shorter-lived animals. The ages shown in the age boxes are the average natural life spans of the animals.

Wild animals do not always live their full natural life span. Other animals, including humans, hunt and kill them. If an animal is injured it may not be able to

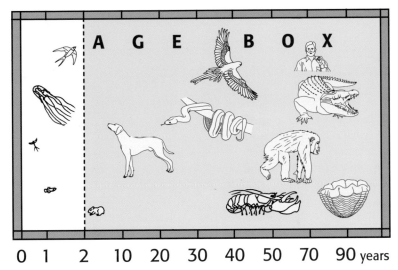

These scale boxes give an idea of how long the animals live in comparison to each other. A human being is also included.

feed itself and will die. Animals are also suffer from **drought**, and often their homes are destroyed by people. Animals sometimes live longer in zoos or wildlife parks, where they are well-fed and protected. In these cases, the zoo becomes the animal's last refuge. You can see the places where the animals talked about here live. Turn to pages 30 and 31 in the back of this book.

The Mayfly

On warm summer evenings the air above ponds and streams swarms with flying insects that live no more than a day. They have a large pair of glistening, veined forewings, and a much smaller pair of wings set behind. These delicate creatures are mayflies. There are almost 1,500 species of mayfly that live around the world.

Adult mayflies mate in midair, and some species perform aerial dances. They lay their eggs in or on fresh water. Soon after this both the male and female die. The eggs hatch into nymphs and they feed on tiny plants and animals in the water.

A young mayfly, called a nymph, is wingless and lives for up to three years underwater. It breathes through **gills** and **molts** several times as it grows. At first, the mayfly is dull in color and cannot mate. But soon it casts its skin again, and the perfect adult mayfly appears. This usually begins to happen in May. That is why it is called a mayfly.

Mayfly

Enemies

Birds, such as swallows and martins, love to eat mayflies. So do fish. Anglers make fake mayflies as bait for trout.

Going Hungry

Mayflies cannot eat during their entire adult lives because their mouthparts are almost useless.

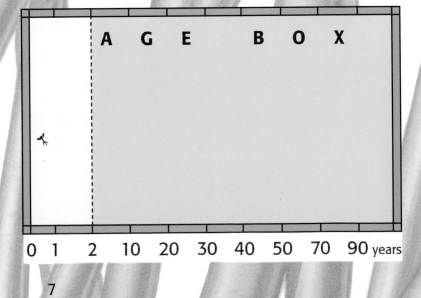

A G E   B O X

0 1   2   10   20   30   40   50   70   90 years

The Killifish

There are about 300 different kinds of killifish, tiny minnowlike fish. These fish live in warm, fresh or salt water around the world. Some kinds of killifish that live in Africa and South America have very short lives. In fact, these have the shortest lives of all fish.

Scientists call these killifish "annual fish" because their life span is very short. From birth, through mating, to death, is usually less than a year. It is sometimes as little as eight months. This is because they live in shallow water in hot places.

During the dry season, when the water begins to evaporate under the blazing sun, the fish lay eggs in the mud beneath the water. When the water has nearly gone, the parents die, but the eggs, still held under the mud, survive in the moisture. Then, the rainy season begins again and water returns. Now the eggs hatch into baby fish that quickly grow into adults, but they, too, will die in the next drought. And so the cycle goes on and on.

A Fish in a Footprint

Some killifish spend their short lives in very little water. They can survive in ditches, tiny ponds, and even in the water-filled footprints of large animals, such as zebras and buffalo.

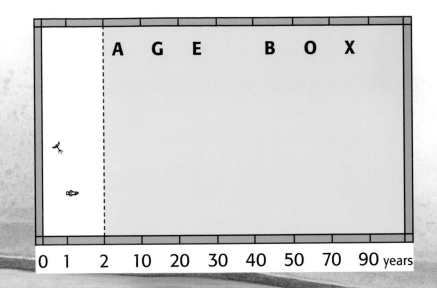

A G E   B O X

0   1   2   10   20   30   40   50   70   90 years

PRETTY AND USEFUL

Killifish include pretty-colored species popular with aquarium owners. Other killifish, such as the strangely named mummichog of the eastern United States, are very useful. This is because they keep down the number of mosquitoes by eating their young.

Killifish

The Jellyfish

Sea Wasp

The jellyfish family has lived in
oceans all over the world for over
600 million years. Some of their cousins,
the sea anemones, live for up to 90 years
or more. Most small jellyfish live less than
one year.

Jellyfish are animals, but they are not fish.
They have no skeleton. Instead, jellyfish have
a soft, umbrella-shaped body, which is really just
a stomach with a mouth on the underside. Some
jellyfish have an umbrella that is four times bigger than
the umbrellas we use in the rain. Others have an umbrella
the size of a child's thumbnail.

A jellyfish's mouth is surrounded by a fringe of delicate, sticky
strands. These strands, called tentacles, can be very long. Some
jellyfish have tentacles that trail through the water for many feet.
These tentacles sting, and the jellyfish use them to paralyze or kill their
prey. Small ocean creatures such as fish, worms, baby shrimp, and even
other jellyfish are the jellyfish's prey.

A Jelly Snack

Loggerhead turtles are not bothered by jellyfish tentacles. They love to eat them, even though the sting makes their eyes sore!

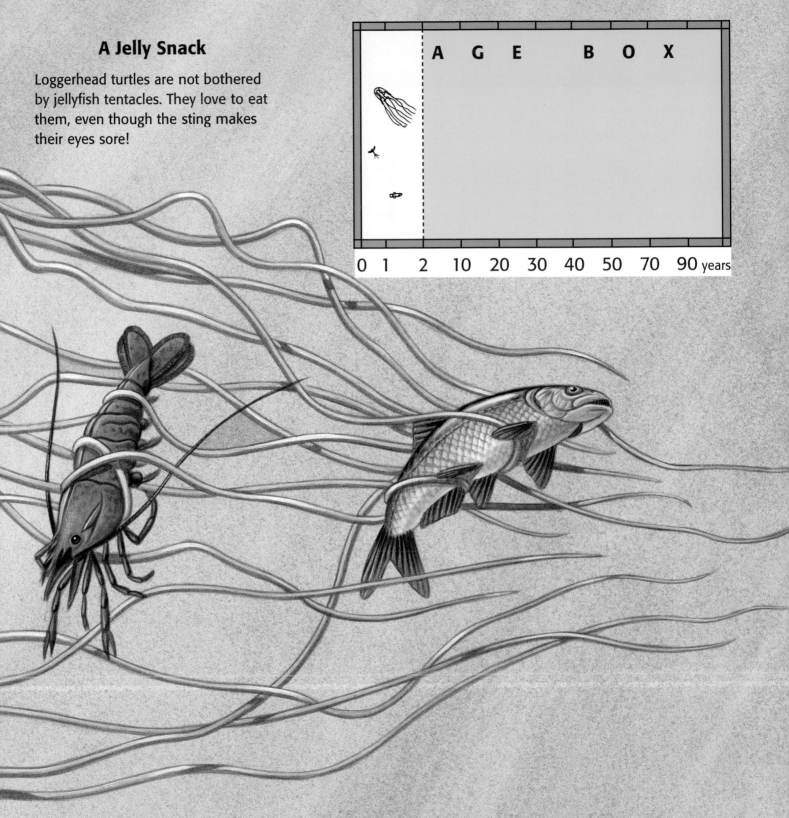

A G E   B O X

0 1   2   10   20   30   40   50   70   90 years

No Brains

Jellyfish are made up mostly of water. Not only do they have no skeleton, they have no brain and no heart either! But they do have muscles and nerves.

Deadly Tentacles

Some jellyfish have very poisonous stings. The most dangerous one is the box jelly, also called the sea wasp. It lives in tropical seas, and its sting can kill human swimmers.

The Swallow

These elegant fliers of the summer skies are among the shortest-lived of all birds. The North American tree swallow, for example, lives an average of only 2.7 years.

Swallows nest in holes in trees or in the ground. Some swallows dig out their nests in sandy banks. Or they build their nests in the burrows of other animals and birds, such as kingfishers or aardvarks. Swallows make nests in and on houses and other buildings, too. Their nests are made of mud, which both the male and female carry in their bills to the nesting site. They arrange and model the mud into a bowl shape, adding bits of straw and twigs. Then the swallows line it with dry grass and feathers. It takes about one week and a thousand mouthfuls of mud to build a nest.

There are 76 different kinds of swallows. They live almost everywhere in the world. Eight kinds of swallows, including the familiar barn swallow, live in North America.

Barn swallow

Life in the Air

Swallows feed on insects that they catch in mid-flight. They also drink while flying across the surface of a river or pond. They just dip their bills briefly into the water. Swallows spend much of their time flying, mostly in flocks, and hardly ever land on the ground. You often see them perched on buildings and telephone wires.

A G E   B O X

0 1 2 10 20 30 40 50 70 90 years

A Long Journey

North American swallows spend the winter in Mexico and Central America. They return to the United States and Canada in early spring.

Good Luck

Romans thought that if a swallow nested in a building, it brought good luck.

13

The Hamster

Hamsters are small mammals with soft fur. Their life span is only two to three years, with an average of one and a half to two years. In the wild they live in Asia and southeast Europe. They eat crops and dig burrows that often damage land where food is grown. This makes them unpopular with farmers. Little is known about some species, while others are kept as pets.

There are several different kinds of hamsters, including the Chinese hamster, the European hamster, the tiny Djungarian hamster, and, commonest of all pet hamsters, the golden hamster. Golden hamsters are easy to keep, and they make good pets. They are more active at night than during the day. They do not like having other hamsters around, except in the breeding season.

Hamsters in the Wild

Hamsters are related to rats and mice. They live in open country and hide from enemies in their burrows. They come out at night to look for grain, seeds, and plants. What a hamster cannot eat, it carries back to the burrow in its mouth. Some hamsters that live in cold places sleep through the winter.

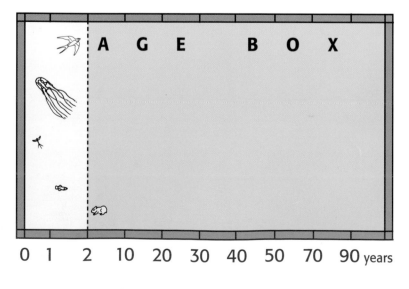

A G E B O X

0 1   2   10 20 30 40 50 70 90 years

14

A Golden Find

In 1930 a scientist from Jerusalem found a female golden hamster and 11 young in a burrow 6.5 feet (2 meters) deep in Syria. He took some of the young away with him to breed them. Many of the pet golden hamsters in the world today come from that original hamster and her young.

Golden hamster

The Dog

Most dogs live for over ten years. These larger breeds tend to age more quickly than small breeds. Great Danes, for example, are getting old at eight or nine years. Few will live beyond 11 or 12 years. Smaller dogs, such as terriers, can live for 20 years.

Dalmatians might live for anything between 11 and 16 years. They were originally hunting and herding dogs in southeast Europe. They were brought to England in the 1800s and trained to run alongside carriages. Because of this, they were often known as carriage dogs.

Hot-Water Bottles

A dog's temperature is higher than a human being's. In the days before central heating, people often kept small dogs to keep them warm. The dogs would sit on people's laps, and so, became called lap dogs.

A Dog's Life

Pet dogs should always have good quality food and plenty of exercise. With good care, pet dogs can live long and happy lives. One of the record holders for a long life was a cocker spaniel in Ohio. It died in 1974 at the age of 29 years.

Toy dogs

Toy dogs, such as Pekinese and Yorkshire terriers, are small, pretty dogs that have been specially bred as pets. They tend to have shorter life spans than other small dogs.

All dogs are related to the wolf. Between 10,000 and 35,000 years ago humans began to keep dogs to help them hunt. People tamed them and bred them for work, and also kept them as pets. There are many kinds of pet dogs, but some dogs still live in the wild. They hunt other animals for food, although some wild dogs also eat mushrooms, nuts, and fruits.

Dalmatian

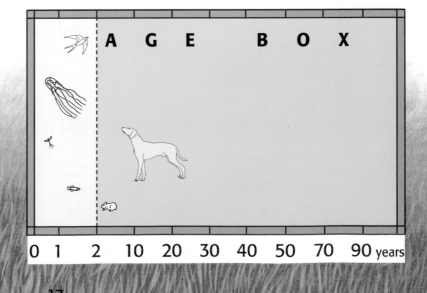

A G E   B O X

0   1   2   10   20   30   40   50   70   90 years

The Snake

Some snakes can live for 40 years, although they don't live as long as other reptiles, such as the tortoise and the crocodile. African cobras and the Northern copperheads of the United States, both poisonous snakes, can live for almost 30 years. The big constrictor snakes can live for about 40 years. They are not poisonous, but kill their prey by coiling around them so that they cannot breathe. These giant snakes include the anaconda and boa constrictor of South America, the reticulated python of tropical Asia, and the amethystine python of Australia and the Philippines.

Snakes grow rapidly during the first few years of life. How much they grow after this depends upon what food they can find and how active they are. Like crocodiles, they grow much more, and more quickly, when they are young. They grow very slowly, if at all, when they are old. Most snakes eat meat, from earthworms and insects to large mammals, such as antelopes. Some snakes eat eggs—shells and all! They swallow their food whole because they cannot chew it.

Scales and Fingernails

A snake's scales are made out of the same material as your hair and fingernails. This material is called keratin.

Snakes live around the world, in trees and burrows, in deserts and forests. There are no snakes in New Zealand, Ireland, Iceland or near the North and South Poles.

Indian python

Snakes and Dragons

There are many legends and superstitions about snakes. At one time people believed in dragons. These were thought to be fire-breathing, scaly creatures that lived in the underground guarding huge piles of precious stones. Scaly snakes that live in the dark and have flickering tongues may have inspired these stories. People also once believed that snakes could live for a thousand years. This idea may have come from the way these reptiles crawl out of their old skin and look young again.

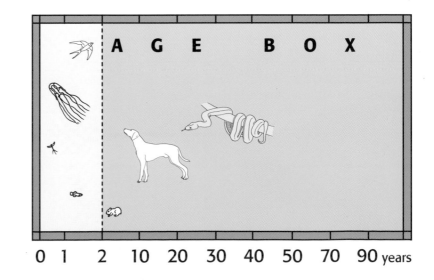

A G E B O X

0 1   2   10   20   30   40   50   70   90 years

The Parrot

Some birds, such as swallows and robins, are short-lived. Others can live as long as the longer-lived mammals. Parrots, particularly the larger species, live for between 30 and 50 years. Some of them, kept as pets or in zoos, have even lived for 80 years.

There are about 315 species of parrots. They live in flocks, ususally in **tropical** forests. Male and females form pairs that stay together for most of their lives. The upper half of a parrot's beak is hooked and curves downward. The lower half of its beak is smaller and curves upward. The two halves form a powerful nut and seed cracker and a third "foot" that they use for climbing. Parrots have one-of-a-kind feet. Two outer toes point backward, and two inner toes point forward. This helps them grip things strongly. They can handle things with more skill than other birds.

A Beautiful Blue

Many parrots are brightly colored, beautiful birds. One of the biggest and most beautiful parrots is the hyacinth macaw of South America. This bird has magnificent blue feathers.

Natural Dangers

Between 60 and 75 percent of all birds die between the ages of three and six months old from starvation, disease, or being eaten by other animals.

Hyacinth macaw

A G E B O X

0 1 2 10 20 30 40 50 70 90 years

The Lobster

The lobster has a hard shell. From time to time it casts off its shell, and a bigger one forms on the soft body underneath. This casting off or molting happens less often as it gets older. The bigger the lobster, the older it is. Very large American lobsters can live up to 50 years. American lobsters live along the Atlantic coast of the United States. Other lobsters live along rocky coasts all over the world.

A young lobster swims freely for the first 12 days of its life. Then it goes down to the seafloor. Here it spends the rest of its life in undersea caves or sunken wrecks. At night the lobster feeds on live and dead fish, small shellfish, seaweed, and sometimes other lobsters.

American lobster

Crushing Claws

Some of the bigger species of lobsters, such as the American lobster, can weigh as much as a small dog. They have crushing claws that are powerful enough to break a person's wrist.

No Bones

Lobsters are crustaceans. This means that they do not have a skeleton inside their bodies, but their tough shell acts as a protective outer skeleton. They have jointed legs, gills for breathing, and feelers or antennae that they use for "tasting" the watery world around them.

Natural Colors

When European and American lobsters are alive, they are dark green or blue. They only turn red when cooked. Because so many lobsters are caught for food there are fewer of them around the world. Pollution has also killed many lobsters.

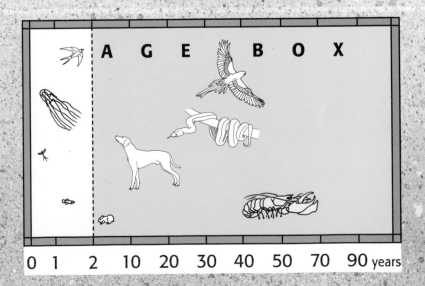

A G E   B O X

| 0 | 1 | 2 | 10 | 20 | 30 | 40 | 50 | 70 | 90 years |

Chimpanzee

Handy Chimps

Chimpanzees are very clever tool-users. They push twigs into termite nests and then pull them out covered with crawling insects. Chimpanzees also make cups out of leaves.

24

The Chimpanzee

You might think that the life span of a chimpanzee would be similar to that of a human. That is not quite true. Although chimpanzees can live to be 60, very few pass their fiftieth birthday. They seem to live longer in zoos than in the wild. But, as you know, life for the animal in the zoo may not truly be good for the animal.

There are two species of chimpanzees. They are the common chimpanzee and pygmy chimpanzee. Both species live in the tropical forests and open woodland of West and Central Africa. They usually form small groups of 20 or fewer that make up larger communities in a territory.

Chimpanzees, together with gorillas and orangutans, are our closest living relatives. Like us, they belong to the group of mammals called primates. Other primates include lemurs, bush babies, monkeys, and gibbons.

Old Age

Old chimpanzees may develop rheumatism, lose hair, and become hard of hearing, just like elderly humans.

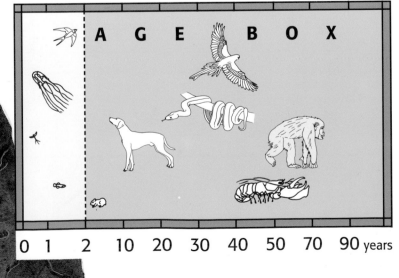

AGE BOX

0 1 2 10 20 30 40 50 70 90 years

Sleep Like a Bird

Chimpanzees will look for food on the ground. But they spend most of their time in trees. At night they make themselves a comfortable nest of branches and leaves to sleep in.

25

Tooth Picks

Crocodiles cool themselves in the sun by lying with their mouths open. This also allows birds to come and pick rotting food from between their teeth.

Saltwater crocodile

Huge Ancestors

Crocodiles have been around since before the days of the dinosaurs. The oldest **fossil** of a primitive crocodile dates back to about 200 million years ago. This fossil was found in what is now Argentina. The fossil skulls from ancient crocodiles are as long as an adult man is tall. Their bodies stretch almost the length of a tennis court! These monsters probably hunted young dinosaurs.

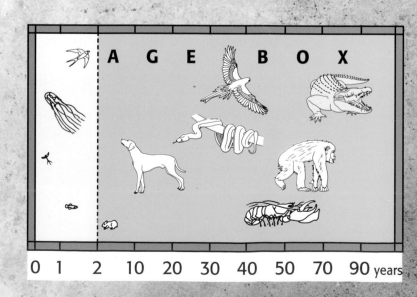

A G E B O X

0 1 2 10 20 30 40 50 70 90 years

The Crocodile

Crocodiles and their close relatives, the alligators, live in warm parts of the world. They live in rivers, lakes, and at the edge of the ocean. Not much is known about how long they live in the wild. We do know that some captive alligators have lived 50 to 100 years. Unlike mammals and birds, crocodiles and alligators may continue to grow, although very slowly of course, when they are old.

There are 21 species of crocodiles and alligators in the world. The largest is the saltwater crocodile. It can reach about 25 feet (8 m) in length and weigh about 2.2 tons (2 mt). A few crocodile species, including the saltwater one, will sometimes, but very rarely, attack and eat humans.

Crocodiles and alligators are reptiles—**cold-blooded** animals. This means that their body temperature changes with the surrounding air or water. They breathe air with lungs, have with bony skeletons inside, and their skin is covered with protective scales or plates. Their young hatch from eggs with a leathery waterproof shell. Most reptiles lay their eggs on land. In some species, the eggs are kept inside the mother's body until the young hatch.

The Clam

You might guess that animals that just sit still, waiting for food to come to them, would live to a ripe old age. This is certainly true of some clams. The biggest clam is the giant clam. It lives for 80 years or more in shallow tropical waters. Its shell can grow as wide as the outstretched arms of a nine-year-old child. It can weigh as much as two fully-grown men.

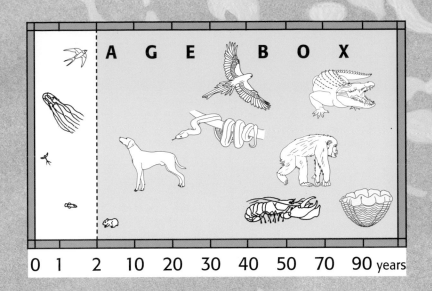

A G E   B O X

| 0 | 1 | 2 | 10 | 20 | 30 | 40 | 50 | 70 | 90 | years |

A clam that lives even longer than the giant clam is the tiny deep-sea clam, tindaria. It takes about a hundred years to grow to the size of a pea!

Clams belong to the big group of animals called mollusks. Because they have two shells, clams are called bivalves. Mollusks with just one shell are called univalves. Snails are an example of a univalve, a shell with only one valve. Some mollusks, the slug and the octopus for example, don't have a shell at all.

Giant clam

Priceless Pearl

The biggest pearl ever found, the Pearl of Laotze, came from a giant clam. It is as big as a house brick and weighs 14 pounds (6.5 kg). It was last valued at over $4 million.

A pearl is made when something, such as a piece of sand or grit, gets inside the shell of a mollusk. The creature makes a shiny hard material to cover the grit to protect itself. This builds up to become a pearl. Not all pearls are considered valuable. The shiny, pretty pearls used in jewelry come from another bivalve, the oyster.

29

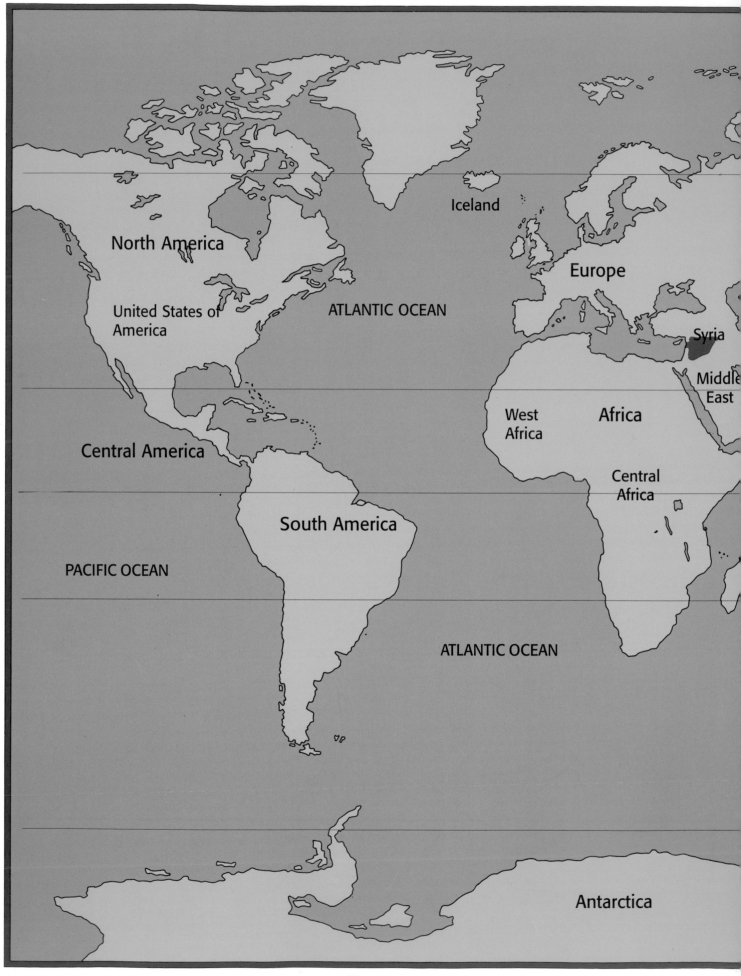

North America

Iceland

Europe

United States of
America

ATLANTIC OCEAN

Syria

Middle
East

West
Africa

Africa

Central America

Central
Africa

South America

PACIFIC OCEAN

ATLANTIC OCEAN

Antarctica

Glossary

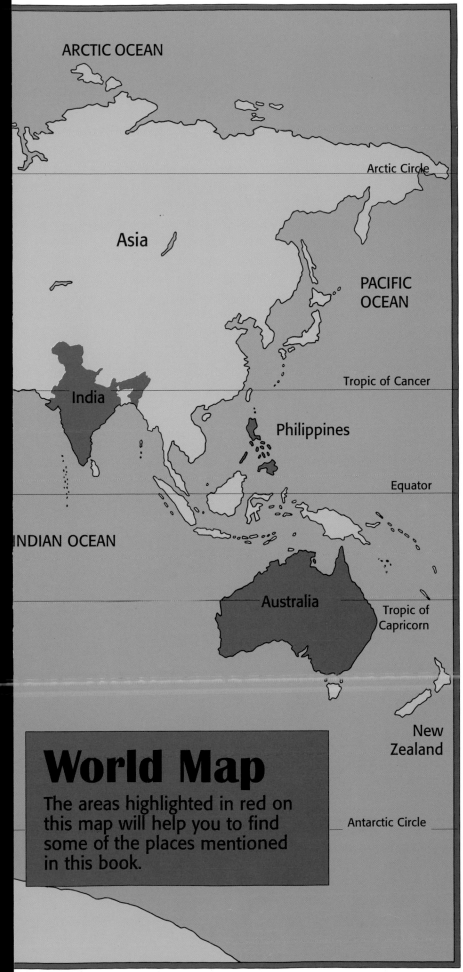

ARCTIC OCEAN

Arctic Circle

Asia

PACIFIC
OCEAN

Tropic of Cancer

India

Philippines

Equator

INDIAN OCEAN

Australia

Tropic of
Capricorn

New
Zealand

Antarctic Circle

World Map

The areas highlighted in red on this map will help you to find some of the places mentioned in this book.

bacterium A one-celled creature that is too small to be seen without a microscope. If there is more than one bacterium, they are called **bacteria**.

cells The smallest living parts of the body. All living plants and animals are made up of cells.

cold-blooded Animals whose body temperature changes with the air or water around them.

drought A long period of time when there is no rain. Plants die and water holes dry up.

fossil The remains of a dead animal or plant that has changed into stone over millions of years.

gills Delicate sheets of cells that take in oxygen from water. Fish and some other animals that live in water use gills instead of lungs to breathe.

life span The length of life of a plant or animal.

microscopic Too tiny to be seen without using a scientific instrument called a microscope. A microscope magnifies things.

molt To shed the outer skin, or, in some animals, hair or feathers.

pigment A colored chemical.

species A group of animals or plants that are closely related.

tropical Found on or near the tropics. Tropical areas of the world are hot all the year round. They have a rainy season and a dry season.

Index

Numbers in **bold** refer to illustrations. Words in **bold** appear in the glossary on page 31.

A
Africa 8, 25, **30**
alligator 27
amethystine python 18
antenna 23
Asia 14, 18, **31**
Atlantic 22, **30**
Australia 18, **31**

B
bacteria 4, 31
barn swallow **12-13**
birds 3, 6, 12, 13, 20, 21, 26
birth 3, 8, 27
boa constrictor 18
breeding 14, 15
burrows 14, 15, 18

C
cells 4, 31
chimpanzee 4, 24-25
    common **24-25**
    pygmy 25
clam
    giant clam **28-29**
    tindaria 29
claws 22
cobra 18
cold-blooded 27, 31
common shrew 3
crocodile 18, 26-27
    saltwater 8, **26-27**
crustacean 23

D
dinosaurs 26
dogs 4, 16-17, 22
    Dalmatian **16-17**
drought 5, 8, 31

E
eggs 6, 8, 27
Europe 14, 16, **30**

F
feathers 20
feeding 6, 7, 12, 14, 16, 17, 18, 22
fish 6, 8, 9, 10
fossils 26, 31

G
gills 6, 23, 31
gorilla 25

H
hamster **14-15**
heartbeats 3-4

I
Iceland 18, **30**
Ireland 18, **30**

J
jellyfish 10-11
    sea wasp (box jelly) **10-11**

K
keratin 18
killifish **8-9**

L
life span 3, 5, 8, 12, 14, 17, 25, 31
lobster 22
    American **22-23**
    European 23

M
macaw 20
mammals 3, 14, 20, 25
mating 6, 8
mayfly **6-7**
microscopic 4, 31
mollusks 29
molt 6, 22, 31
mouth 7, 10, 26

N
nests 12, 13, 25
New Zealand 18, **31**
North America 12, 18, **30**

O
old age 4
orangutan 25

P
parrot 20-21
    hyacinth macaw **20-21**
pearl 29
pets 14, 16, 17, 20
Philippines 18, **31**
pigment 4, 31
pollution 23
primates 25
python 18

Q
Queen termite 4

R
rainy season 8
reptiles 18, 19, 27
reticulated python 18
rheumatism 25

S
sea anemones 10
scales 18, 27
shell 22, 23, 29
skeleton 10, 11, 23, 27
snakes 18-19
    Indian python **18-19**
South America 8, 18, 20, **30**
species 3, 20, 27, 31
swallow 6, 12-13, 20

T
tentacles 10, 11
tortoises 3, 18
tropical 11, 20, 25, 28, 31

U
US 9, 18, 22, **30**

Z
zoos 3, 5, 20, 25